OneRepublic

dreaming out loud

ISBN 978-1-4234-4346-9

HAL•LEONARD®
CORPORATION
7777 W. BLUEMOUND RD. P.O. BOX 13819 MILWAUKEE, WI 53213

Visit Hal Leonard Online at
www.halleonard.com

SAY
(All I Need)

Words and Music by RYAN TEDDER, EDDIE FISHER,
ZACK FILKINS, BRENT KUTZLE and ANDREW BROWN

Moderately slow

Do you know where your heart ____ is? Do you think you can find ____ it? Or did you trade it for some - thing some - where?

MERCY

Words and Music by RYAN TEDDER
and ANDREW BROWN

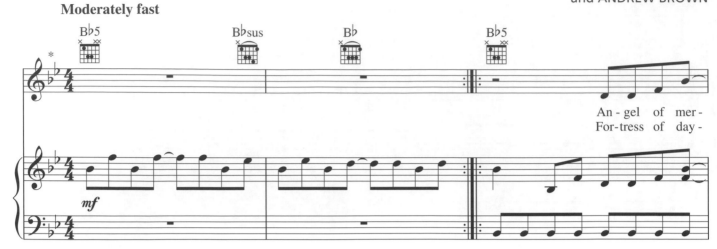

An - gel of mer-
For - tress of day-

- cy, how did you find _____ me? Where did you read _____
- light, caught me on stand - by wait - ing to catch _____

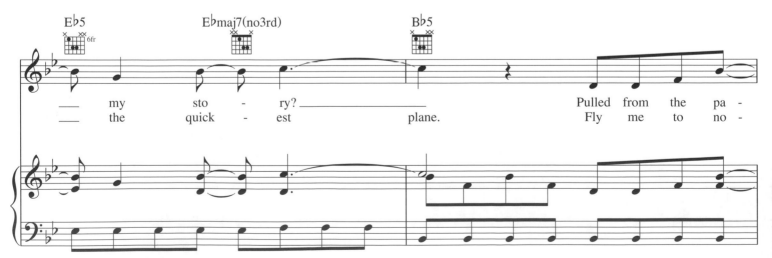

_____ my sto - ry? _____ Pulled from the pa -
_____ the quick - est plane. Fly me to no -

Recorded a half step higher.

STOP AND STARE

Words and Music by RYAN TEDDER,
ANDREW BROWN, TIM MYERS,
ZACK FILKINS and EDDIE FISHER

APOLOGIZE

Words and Music by
RYAN TEDDER

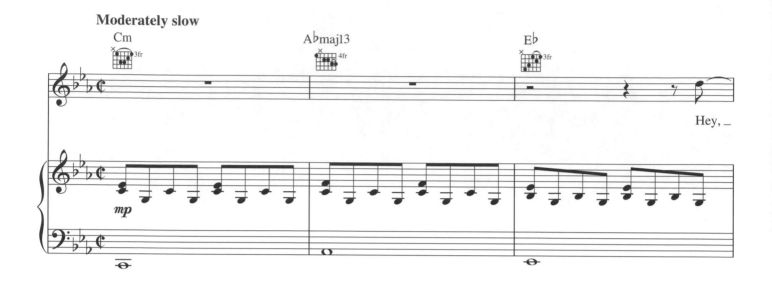

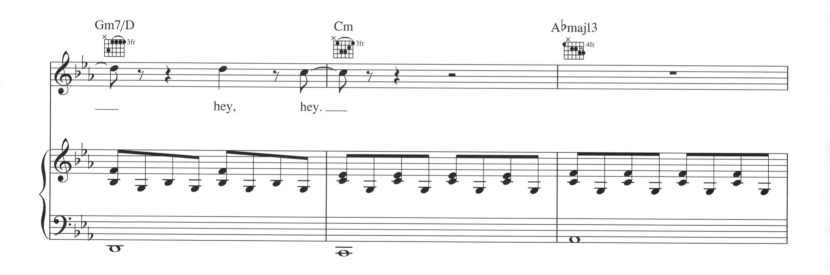

GOODBYE APATHY

Words and Music by
RYAN TEDDER

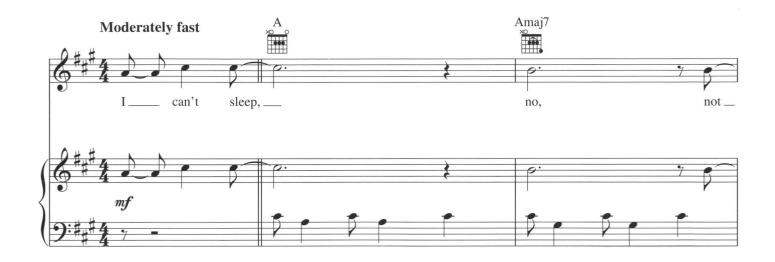

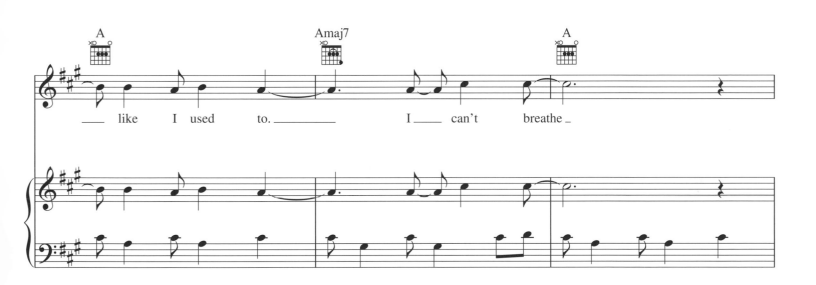

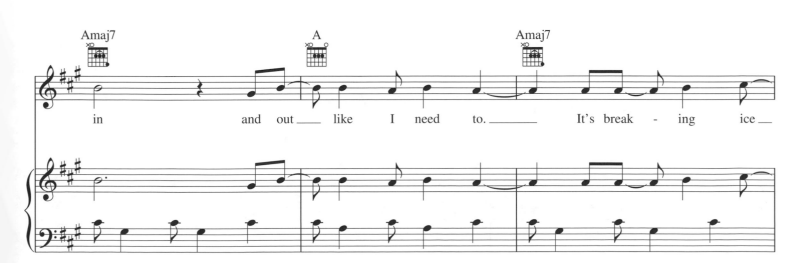

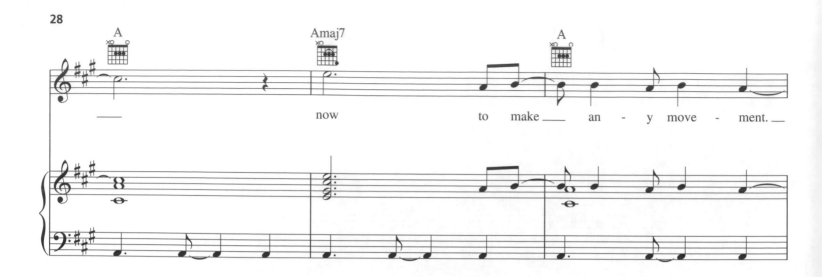

now to make an - y move - ment.

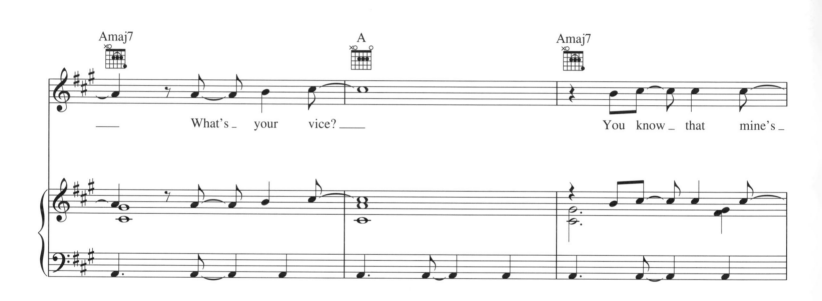

What's _ your vice? _____ You know _ that mine's _

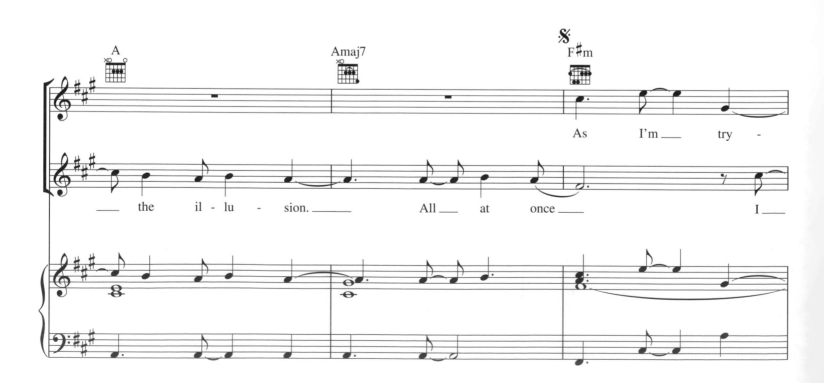

_____ the il - lu - sion. _____ All at once _____ I _____ As I'm _____ try -

ALL FALL DOWN

Words and Music by RYAN TEDDER, EDDIE FISHER,
ZACK FILKINS, BRENT KUTZLE and ANDREW BROWN

Step out the door _
God love your soul _

_ and it feels like rain. _ That's the sound, that's the sound on your win-dow - pane. _
_ and your ach - ing bones. _ Take a breath, take a step, meet me down be - low. _

TYRANT

Words and Music by RYAN TEDDER,
ANDREW BROWN and ZACK FILKINS

Moderately fast

Watch - in' my - self,___ and I'm tak - ing strides,___

Half tempo

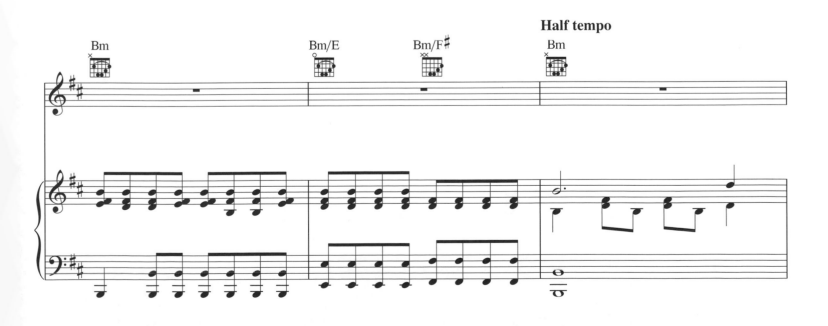

PRODIGAL

Words and Music by RYAN TEDDER, TIM MYERS,
ANDREW BROWN, ZACK FILKINS and JERROD BETTIS

WON'T STOP

Words and Music by RYAN TEDDER, EDDIE FISHER,
ZACK FILKINS, BRENT KUTZLE and ANDREW BROWN

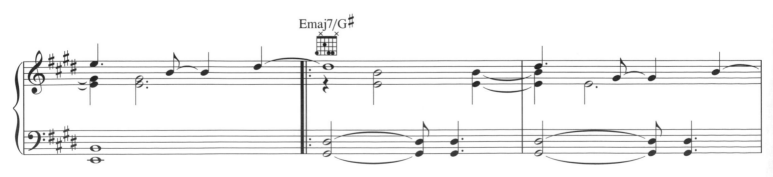

love ain't __ fair, _____ but I'm do - ing fine, _
fool your - self; _____ this is my _____ truth. _

'cause

I swear _ it's you, I swear _ it's

you, I swear _ it's you that I've

Bsus
B(add4)
wait - ed for. And I swear it's
Amaj9
you, I swear it's you,
C♯m11
I swear it's you that my heart beats for,
Bsus
B(add4)
D6/9
and it ain't gon - na stop,

(Vocals ad lib. to end)

ALL WE ARE

Words and Music by RYAN TEDDER
and TIM MYERS

Moderately slow

mf

I tried to paint you a pic -
I walked a min - ute in your __

- ture; the col - ors were __ all wrong. __ Black and white __ did - n't fit __
__ shoes; they nev - er would have fit. ____ I fig - ured there's __ noth - ing to __

__ you, and all a - long __ you were shad - ed with pa -
__ lose; I need to get __ some per - spec - tive on these __

76

SOMEONE TO SAVE YOU

Words and Music by RYAN TEDDER,
TIM MYERS and EDDIE FISHER

Hon - es - ty   is what you need;   it

sets you free _____ like some - one to save ____ you.

Let it go,   but hur - ry, though.   There's

un - der - tow   and I don't wan - na lose ____ you now. ____

COME HOME

Words and Music by
RYAN TEDDER

Am

the bet - ter half of me. _____ They're in the

well, hope-ful - ly the hate _____ sub - sides and the love can _ be - gin. _

Fmaj7

Dm

wrong place, try - in' to make _ it right, _____ but

It might _____ start _____ now, _____ or

G

Dm

I'm tired of jus - ti - fy - ing. So I say _ to you:

may - be I'm just dream - ing out loud. _____ Well, un - til _____ then, _

G

Am

C

come home, _ come home, _____ 'cause I've been wait - ing for _____

Em/B

F